The Early People of Florida

BOOKS BY EVA DEUTSCH COSTABEL

New England Village

The Pennsylvania Dutch

The Jews of New Amsterdam

The Early People of Florida

The Early People of Florida

Eva Deutsch Costabel

ATHENEUM 1993
New York

Maxwell Macmillan Canada
Toronto

Maxwell Macmillan International
New York   Oxford   Singapore   Sydney

I dedicate this book to the six million Jewish martyrs—men, women, and children, my brothers and sisters—who were murdered during the Holocaust.

Many thanks to Eugene Lyon, director of the Center for Historic Research at Flagler College, for taking time to check my manuscript and artwork and for his valuable advice. He demonstrated great generosity and kindness by letting me use his office and his research papers, even though I was a stranger from New York.

Also my thanks to Susan L. Clark of the Historic Saint Augustine Preservation Board, Cookie O'Brien at Historic Saint Augustine, and Lincoln Dexter.

Atheneum
Macmillan Publishing Company
866 Third Avenue
New York, NY 10022

Maxwell Macmillan Canada, Inc.
1200 Eglinton Avenue East
Suite 200
Don Mills, Ontario M3C 3N1

Macmillan Publishing Company is part of the Maxwell Communication Group of Companies.

First edition
Printed in Hong Kong

1 2 3 4 5 6 7 8 9 10

Library of Congress Cataloging-in-Publication Data
Costabel, Eva Deutsch.
The early people of Florida / written and illustrated by Eva Deutsch Costabel.—1st ed.
p.   cm.
Summary: Discusses the origins, way of life, and history of the early people who settled in Florida thousands of years before the arrival of the first Europeans.
ISBN 0-689-31500-7
1. Indians of North America—Florida—History—Juvenile literature. 2. Indians of North America—Florida—First contact with Europeans—Juvenile literature. 3. Indians of North America—Florida—Antiquities—Juvenile literature. 4. Florida—Discovery and exploration—Juvenile literature. [1. Indians of North America—Florida—History. 2. Indians of North America—Florida—Antiquities. 3. Florida—Discovery and exploration.] I. Title.
E78.F6C67   1993
975.9'00497—dc20   92-16283

Contents

Florida's Prehistoric Past   1
The Earliest People
The Mount Taylor People
The Orange Pottery Period
The Saint Johns People

Native Americans in Florida   8

Juan Ponce de León   12

Pánfilo de Narváez   16

Hernando de Soto   17

Early Missions and Settlements   19

The French in Florida   20

Fort Caroline   24

Saint Augustine   27

Santa Elena   28

Changing Hands   32

Bibliography   34

San Felipe
(San Marcos) de
Santa Elena

San Pedro

San Esteban
San Mateo   San Gabriel

San Agustín

Matanzas

TIMUCUA

Tocobaga

Santa Lucía

CALUSA

San Antonio

TEGESTA

Tegesta

Florida's Prehistoric Past

When the first Europeans arrived in Florida, people had been living there for at least fifteen thousand years. Some scientists even think that humans could have been found there as many as fifty thousand years ago. New information about these ancient people is being learned all the time.

The early people banded together in small groups to hunt. Their prey was the gigantic animals of the Ice Age: woolly mammoths, mastodons (early elephants), horses, walrus, giant sloths, camels, bison, and musk-oxen. The earliest hunting grounds were in the upper part of Florida's peninsula, which was covered with forests of hickory, oak, and beech, with open prairies. The animals that lived there, many now extinct, provided early man not only with his food, but with shelter and clothing.

Early people did not survive by hunting only. They also gathered wild plants, searched for berries, and collected nuts. Many also harvested shellfish. They left huge mounds of the shells as early garbage heaps, and much that scientists know about these early people comes from studying the trash they left behind. In these mounds (such as Turtle Mound on Anastasia Island) can be found early tools: stone spears for hunting, various stone knives and scrapers used for preparing meat and skins, and needles made of bone.

For a long time it was believed that these early hunting-gathering people wandered from place to place seeking food. New discoveries seem to show that they might have lived in small huts, formed into villages, where they stayed when they were not hunting. The men might have joined into hunting bands to follow prey, and might have built temporary camps near their hunting ground.

The Earliest People

About six thousand years ago there was a great change in Florida's climate, and it became warmer. Swamps appeared where before there had been dry land, and pines replaced the oak and hickory of the forest. No longer were the giant sloths and mastodons roaming the earth. Deer and other smaller animals now appeared. The way of life changed for the people also, and they had to change their way of hunting. New tools were invented, new types of wild plants were found and gathered. Native Americans migrated from the central highlands to other parts of Florida. Small villages were built in the northeast, and a more permanent way of life began.

Some of the groups moved to coastal regions. Here they lived in more established communities for long periods of the year, and food sources were ample and varied. Native Americans of that period hunted deer, rabbits, and other small mammals, as well as birds and snakes. They gathered freshwater snails, nuts, and edible plants. Tools also changed to adapt to the new way of life. Large spear points were made of chert, which contains quartz, and this material was harder and stronger than the stone used earlier.

Stone scrapers to prepare meat developed into different shapes. A spear thrower, the atlatl, was used in hunting to add distance and power to the spear thrust. Early man also learned to make awls for piercing small holes into leather, wood, and other materials. Chisels and hammers were made out of shell.

The Mount Taylor People

One group of hunters and gatherers of this period, four thousand to six thousand years ago, living in northeast Florida, is called the Mount Taylor People. Much of their history is found in the mounds and earthworks they left behind. They ate great quantities of shellfish—clams, mussels, and sea snails—and the shells they threw away created even greater mounds. Many can still be found in Florida, although others have been destroyed. Some of the mounds were used by the early native Americans as temple sites and burial grounds.

4

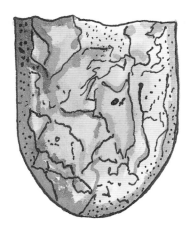
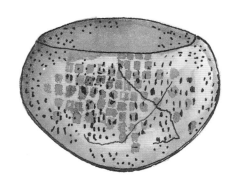

The Orange Pottery Period

About four thousand years ago people moved again, this time to an area of saltwater marshes and inlets along the coastline, where they could find sure supplies of oysters. In this habitat the people learned to make pots and bowls of clay, strengthened with plant fibers. This is the first time pottery appears in the New World.

Fall and winter months were spent in small villages near the coast. There the people collected oysters and small clams and caught turtles and snakes. They also fished and hunted.

In the spring they returned to the Saint Johns River for hunting and food gathering and remained there all summer. About 1200 B.C. the orange-colored pottery disappeared.

The Saint Johns People

About 500 B.C. a new period of culture emerged, and it lasted until the arrival of the Europeans.

Though the life-style of native Americans remained pretty much the same, there were some changes. The population increased, villages grew larger, and people spent longer periods of time in them. In the cooler months of the year, they lived along the marshes and lagoons of the coastline, harvesting oysters for their staple food. They also fished, caught snakes, and hunted deer and birds with the bow and arrow and the spear. They continued to gather nuts, berries, and wild plants, as the people before them did.

As time went on, people learned to grow plants, such as corn, squash, and pumpkins. In the winter they lived in large coastal villages, and when planting time came early in the spring, they moved to coastal waterways and separated into small farming groups. Scarcity of good soil kept the groups small. Most of the information about this period, like that about the other early periods, comes from the shell mounds, which were found on the banks of the Intracoastal Waterways. Some of the mounds reached thirty feet in height and stretched to a mile in length.

Native Americans in Florida

When the first Europeans arrived in Florida, there were at least five thousand to ten thousand native Americans living there, but there might have been even more. The four major groups were the Timucua, who lived in the northeast, the Tequesta in the southeast, the Calusa in the southwest, and the Apalache in the northwest Gulf region.

The Timucua lived in villages of about 20 houses and 150 people. Tall wooden walls were built around the villages to protect them against their enemies. The Timucua were farmers and their staple food was corn.

In the center of the village was the community house, where much of the village public life took place. People gathered there for festivities, religious ceremonies, political events, and all the official business of the community. During the fall harvest the crops were stored here and meat and fish dried on nearby smoking racks.

Much of what we know about the Timucua comes from the drawings of the French artist Jacques de Morgues Le Moyne, who visited Florida in 1560. He was the first European artist to record Florida natives. Le Moyne's party saw in the temples fine wooden sculptures wrapped in colored skins and decorated with plumes and tassels. Chiefs were greatly respected and were carried in elaborate processions.

The Calusa were a people with an advanced culture living in towns and villages along the southwest coast. They were the most hostile toward the European explorers, attacking them as soon

as they landed. Scientists digging on Florida's west coast in swampy areas have found well-preserved, beautiful wooden statues and masks made by the Calusa.

Like the earliest people, who built refuse or midden mounds, the later tribes also built mounds, and they are one of the most important features of all early Florida cultures. There were burial mounds, mounds raised as bases for temples, and mounds used as platforms for the nobles' houses. Mounds were also built as seawalls and for irrigation.

Many places in Florida still have their original native American names, such as Miami, which means "big water"; Ocala, meaning "spring"; and Apalachicola, "place of the ruling people." All these names stand as a testament to the ancient people who lived for thousands of years in the place we call Florida before the first Europeans arrived on the shores of the peninsula.

Juan Ponce de León

Juan Ponce de León discovered Florida for the Europeans in 1513 on Easter Sunday and named it Pascua Florida, honoring the Easter Festival of Flowers. To the Spanish, La Florida comprised all the unknown land of the eastern United States, as far north as Canada.

Ponce de León first came to America on Columbus's second voyage. Later he received permission from the Spanish king to explore and claim an island named Borinquén. He returned to the island with a large group of settlers and renamed it Puerto Rico.

In 1509 Ponce de León became the governor of Puerto Rico, where he ruled until 1512. He was an able governor, but permitted acts of cruelty toward the unfortunate natives still living there. He finally was dismissed as governor, because of rumors about him told to the Spanish king, but he received another royal commission that made him famous.

Ponce de León heard stories of treasures to be found to the north. To make it even more intriguing, there was said to be a fountain that would make old men young again. Ponce de León carefully planned an expedition to this fabulous land. On March 3, 1513, he sailed from Puerto Rico with three ships to begin the new expedition.

Even though by 1502 there was a map of Florida based on the explorations of a Portuguese navigator, it seems that Don Juan was not aware of it. He believed Florida was an island. He landed at the place where Saint Augustine stands today and commemorated the occasion with a colorful ceremony, claiming the land for the Spanish king. As he sailed down the Florida coast, he encountered unusual currents around one point of land and named it "Cape of the Currents," later to be renamed Cape Canaveral. As he continued down around the coast on his quest for his magic island, he stumbled on a whole

group of other islands, inhabited by turtles. The sailors caught the turtles and gathered their eggs, to add to their food supply. They named the islands Dry Tortugas after the Spanish for turtles, tortugas.

When Don Juan reached the Ten Thousand Islands on Florida's southwest coast, he encountered the Calusa, who were terrified by these strange-looking creatures dressed in shining armor. The terror soon eased and the Calusa returned to attack sailors who had rowed to the mainland for needed water and wood.

Ponce de León never discovered his miraculous island, nor his Fountain of Youth. He also never realized that the land he thought was an island was the southeastern part of North America.

Six years later, in 1519, another explorer, Alonso Alvarez de Pinedo, traveled the same route and saw that Florida was indeed a part of a very large continent.

In 1521 Ponce de León returned to Florida planning a settlement on the west coast near where Charlotte Harbor is today. Calusa villagers attacked at once, wounding Don Juan gravely. He was taken to Cuba, where he died, at age sixty-one. He was buried in Puerto Rico.

Pánfilo de Narváez

Seven years later, in 1528, Pánfilo de Narváez also attempted to settle western Florida. He sailed into Tampa Bay with two ships carrying four hundred men and eighty horses. Narváez and his men lost their way on an expedition inland and could not find their way back to their anchored ships. They were forced to build new ones. They made tools out of their steel armor and jewelry. Horses' manes and tails were cut and used to make rope. Sailors' shirts became sails for the new ships.

Finally they were close to starving and were forced to kill their horses for food. Then once they set sail they encounterd stormy weather. Out of the four hundred men who started with Narváez, only four survived. These four men, enduring great hardships, marched across the North American continent to finally reach civilization in Mexico.

Hernando de Soto

Hernando de Soto, a wealthy aristocrat, organized an even larger expedition of ten ships to settle Florida. He took with him about 700 men, 223 horses, and 300 hogs and other livestock. The ships landed in Florida on May 30, 1539, just about where Tampa is today. Men dressed in shining armor accompanied by the blare of trumpets charged out of their ships with spears ready.

This display terrified the native Americans on shore. They abandoned their villages and withdrew into the interior. De Soto and his men occupied the deserted village, and de Soto moved into the chief's house. There he wrote a letter to the Spanish king describing the events and the country. This is probably the first letter ever to be written from North America.

De Soto was able to rescue Juan Ortiz,

a man from the Narváez party, who had been taken prisoner by native Americans and tortured. He then marched northward in the hope of finding gold as Spanish adventurers had in Peru and Mexico. He did not find any treasure but did find the place where Narváez had slaughtered his horses, and named it the "Bay of Horses." He also discovered Pensacola Bay, and the group spent the winter where Tallahassee is today, celebrating the very first Christmas in North America. They left Florida in spring for further explorations, never to return. De Soto's new ventures took him northwest, where he was the first European to sight the Mississippi River.

For three years de Soto searched farther and farther west, hoping to find his fortune. In his frantic search for treasure, he mistreated and enslaved native Americans everywhere he went, pressuring them for information about the lands where he could find riches. Native Americans, realizing the danger they were in, gave him false information. Finally discouraged, he planned to return to the Mississippi and then to Cuba, to try again the next year.

In March 1542 he camped near the Mississippi River. Three years of frustrated hopes and exhausting marches had taken their toll. He died there in a hut near the river. His three hundred men, the remains of the original seven hundred, returned to Cuba.

Early Missions and Settlements

In 1549 Luis Cancer de Barbastro led a group of Spanish Dominican friars to open a mission in western Florida. This brave attempt ended in tragedy when native Americans massacred the missionaries. Then in 1592, twelve Franciscan monks arrived in Saint Augustine. They succeeded in building twenty missions in five years. One group of missions stretched two hundred miles north from Saint Augustine, and the other extended westward toward the Apalachicola River.

In 1559 an attempt at colonization was organized by Don Tristán de Luna y Arellano, who landed thirteen ships with sixteen hundred people at what is now Pensacola. A hurricane destroyed most of the ships and supplies. After a year the settlers finally moved to Mexico.

The French in Florida

When Spain became wealthy through her discoveries of the Americas, other European countries looked for their opportunity to profit from the riches of the New Continents. Florida was visited by other Spanish expeditions besides those of Ponce de León, Pánfilo de Narváez, and Hernando de Soto. Finally King Philip II of Spain grew tired of sending expeditions to this new continent, where his people encountered massacre, hunger, disease, and hurricanes, and found no gold.

At this time Europe was in the midst of a religious war. Followers of John Calvin and Martin Luther, Protestants, were spreading their influence over northern Europe. Spain, a Catholic country, considered any spread of Protestantism an act of war.

Jean Ribault, a French Huguenot, and a group of his people settled in Florida with the permission of the French king, Charles IX. King Charles encouraged a colony that he hoped would stop Spain's monoply of New World riches. The Huguenots were French Protestants who were being persecuted in Catholic France. They felt they could find a place to worship freely in this new land.

Ribault made the voyage to the New World in seventy-two days without stop. Sailors before him always anchored at the islands along the way, to rest and replenish their supply of water and fresh food.

As Ribault's group traveled up the Florida coast, they passed many rivers, one of which Ribault named "River of May," to honor May Day, 1562. He had brought with him a marble monument engraved with King Charles's name, which would officially mark the French

presence in Florida.

Ribault's ships sailed into Port Royal Sound, in what is today South Carolina, north of the attempted Spanish settlements. There the Huguenots built a wooden fort, naming it Charlesfort. Ribault erected his marble monument to make it official.

He left thirty of his men there, and then he and René Goulaine de Laudonnière, his second in command, along with the remaining crew, sailed back to Dieppe, France, to gather additional settlers and supplies. In Europe, war between Catholics and Protestants was raging. Dieppe was surrounded and Laudonnière was captured. Ribault decided to seek help from Queen Elizabeth of England, also a Protestant, and hostile to Spain.

Elizabeth promised to help him to return to Florida, but he soon realized that she listened to his tales with the thought of claiming Florida herself. Instead of receiving the promised help, Ribault was arrested and thrown into prison in the Tower of London.

Far away in Florida, the thirty men left behind suffered greatly. They had used up all their supplies and did not know how to grow their own food. Their commander was driven mad by hunger and his men killed him. They elected a new leader, Nicholas Barre. In desperate circumstances, the group built a small vessel to return to France.

All the men crowded into the crudely made ship except seventeen-year-old Guillaume Rouffi, who felt that his chances were better for survival with the local native Americans. The fragile, overloaded boat sailed into the Atlantic. It was then becalmed for twenty-one days, causing the men in it more hardship. They were finally rescued by a passing English ship.

The leader, Nicholas Barre, like Jean Ribault before him, was interviewed by Queen Elizabeth and then thrown into the Tower of London.

Fort Caroline

In 1563 Rene Goulaine de Laudonnière tried to colonize Florida once again. He left with three hundred men and four women. Aboard was Jacques de Morgues Le Moyne, who was the first European artist to record native American life in Florida. Laudonnière's group built Fort Caroline, close to the Saint Johns River.

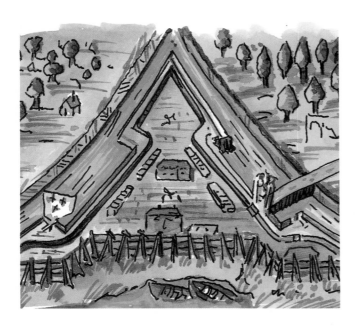

Philip of Spain was angered by the French presence in Florida and sent Captain Hernando Marique de Rojas to force the French out. Rojas sailed in a warship from Havana toward Charlesfort, the French fort that had been built earlier by Ribault. He did not know that the fort had been abandoned. Guillaume Rouffi, the young Frenchman who had remained with native Americans when the French left, led the Spanish captain to Charlesfort. The Spaniard burned the fort to the ground and returned to Havana, convinced that the French had been destroyed.

In the meantime Laudonnière's men at Fort Caroline became restless and discontented. They heard that there was gold and silver in the mountains to the north, and they were eager to go after it. When winter came and supply ships failed to appear, hunger was added to their complaints. They blamed their problems on Laudonnière and plotted to kill him. Their plot was discovered and thirteen rebels escaped in one of the boats. They sailed to Cuba and were captured by a Spanish ship. More men left Laudonnière, and this time they took an even larger boat. Sixty-six men strong, they preyed for a while on Spanish ships in the Caribbean but eventually were also captured.

The men who remained with Laudonnière at Fort Caroline hoped for a vessel to rescue them. A ship finally appeared on the horizon. It was Spanish, but it was soon clear that these were the French rebels, Laudonnière's own men who had escaped Spanish capture. They were hoping for mercy, but Laudonnière had some of them hanged for treason.

In August 1565 more ships appeared in the harbor. Sir John Hawkins, the English sea captain, was cruising Florida waters for treasures from Spanish ships. The French, eager to return to France, struck a deal with the Englishman. The French traded the cannon at Fort Caroline for a ship, food, and supplies. The French were ready to sail, but they needed the right wind. While they waited, another fleet appeared. It was Jean Ribault himself. He had escaped from the Tower of London and had been sent back to Florida with seven ships, supplies, and six hundred sailors, soldiers, and settlers.

The three smallest ships were able to sail to Fort Caroline; the larger ones had to wait at the mouth of the river. A week later a Spanish fleet appeared. Ribault sailed south to attack the Spanish at Saint Augustine, but a hurricane kept him off the coast.

King Philip of Spain had learned of the second attempt of the French to settle in Florida. This time he appointed Pedro Menéndez de Aviles, the finest Spanish naval commander, governor of Florida and sent him to drive out the French for good. Menéndez had sailed across the Atlantic with 18 ships and 1,504 soldiers and settlers, his flagship *San Pelayo* in the lead. The fleet met powerful storms and was delayed, but most of his ships and six hundred people reached Cape Canaveral on August 25, 1565.

They continued north and landed with great pomp at Saint Augustine on September 8, 1565. Menéndez claimed this land for the Spanish crown. Ribault was still delayed off the coast, and Menéndez launched a surprise overland attack on Fort Caroline. The fort was taken in less than one hour, with the loss of 143 Frenchmen. Laudonnière, the artist Le Moyne, and a few others escaped, to be rescued by Ribault's forces. Ribault's main group went on to attack Menéndez, but they were captured and beheaded, ending the French settlement of Florida.

Saint Augustine

Saint Augustine is the oldest continuously occupied city in the United States. On September 8, 1565, Don Pedro Menéndez de Aviles and his ships sailed past Cape Canaveral north of Anastasia Island and landed his group of Spanish settlers. He named the site Saint Augustine because he first sighted shore on that saint's feast day.

The six hundred settlers might not have survived without the help of the local Timucua natives. The Timucua chief Seloy offered the Spaniards their community building for shelter and provided food for the colonists for eighteen months.

But the Spaniards brought diseases with them that killed many of the native Americans, and Spanish men began to take native American wives because there were so few European women among the colonists. Relations between the two groups became tense, and the Spaniards were forced to move to a new settlement across the bay. In 1566 the Jesuit mission was founded nearby, and Jesuit priests traveled throughout all of Florida for thirty years to try to convert the native Americans to Christianity.

The Saint Augustine settlement grew, farms were established, and the colonists were soon producing goods to send back to Spain, goods such as lumber and pitch from the trees, furs, and sassafras root. The first wooden forts were destroyed by fire and rot, and by then the colonists were faced not only with unfriendly natives but with harassment from British colonists in Georgia to the north as well as attacks by pirates.

In 1586 Sir Francis Drake, the English pirate, robbed and burned the town, and in 1668 John Davis, another English pirate, plundered the homes of the citizens once again, killing sixty of the colonists.

Later a local stone, made of seashells, called coquina, was used to rebuild the fort, which was named Castillo de San Marcos. It took fifteen years to construct, but the gate, opened in 1739 and repaired at various times since, is still standing.

In 1740, when England and Spain were at war, the troops from the British colony of Georgia took Anastasia Island and pounded Saint Augustine with cannon fire for thirty days. The residents of the city saved themselves by hiding in the strong new fort.

Santa Elena

On October 7, 1568, three years after the founding of Saint Augustine, two small ships sailed toward Florida. These ships carried 225 new Spanish settlers: men, women, and children to settle at what is now South Carolina's Parris Island. They were mostly small farmers, and Governor Menéndez had promised that their passage would be paid for and that they would be given supplies for two years, including livestock: cows, bulls, oxen, sheep, goats, and chickens. In

return they were to work the land and share the profits with Menéndez. By August 1, 1569, more settlers had arrived, and the city government was formed. The settlers built forty houses on the land given to them. Though most of the people of the colony were farmers, there were also a doctor and a tailor among the group.

By 1571 Menéndez's wife joined him at Santa Elena. He had named it the capital of Spanish Florida, which included all of the eastern half of North America. His wife brought with her fine furniture, linens, kitchenware, and silver, planning a very comfortable future. Unfortunately the ship that brought all this finery also brought disease, and many died from what is now thought to have been typhus.

After this, though, Santa Elena's citizens began to thrive and to develop a life very much like that of their native Spain. There were many soldiers for protection, but there were also traders, craftsmen, masons, tailors, seamen, carpenters, a barber-surgeon, and a smith. There were noblemen and servants. The farmers raised hogs and grew corn, squash, melons, grapes, and barley.

Then new hostilities with the native Americans arose. Many Spaniards were killed, and the people of Santa Elena had to leave their homes and escape to the nearby fort. The attacking natives destroyed the town.

Santa Elena was rebuilt, but it was finally abandoned in 1587 after an English attack. Families were ordered to move to Saint Augustine.

Later the town was rebuilt and the military increased, but after Drake's successful raid on Saint Augustine, the king in Spain decided to concentrate forces there, and Santa Elena was again destroyed, this time by Spanish troops.

Changing Hands

By the end of the sixteenth century the Spanish had built a large settlement on the Gulf Coast at Pensacola to protect the colony from the French in Louisiana, and by 1698 Pensacola was fortified. Then the French took Pensacola from the Spanish in 1719, and in one year the town changed hands four times.

On the east coast, in 1702, Saint Augustine was captured by English settlers from South Carolina, but they could not overcome the defenses at the fort, Castillo de San Marcos, and the attackers had to withdraw. But by 1704 the British, and the native Americans encouraged by them, had been able to destroy a good part of the string of missions the Spanish priests had set up earlier.

In 1739 Spain and England went to war, and in 1740 and 1742 the British governor of Georgia, James Oglethorpe, using many native American troops, took the opportunity to attack Spanish Florida.

There was never peace in the region, and by 1750 England and Spain were at war again. Havana, Cuba, an important Spanish colonial town, was captured by the British. Spain traded all of Florida to Britain for the return of Havana.

So in 1763 Florida became a part of the British colonies and was divided into East Florida with the capital at Saint Augustine and West Florida with Pensacola as the capital. Settlers from the colonies and Europe were encouraged, and many new towns were established, with roads connecting them. Trade increased with the outside world.

When the thirteen English colonies in the north proclaimed independence from England in 1775, the colony of Florida continued to be loyal to the British. In fact, during the Revolution, U.S. patriot prisoners were held in the Castillo de San Marcos in Saint Augustine, and those colonists loyal to the king fled to Florida for safety. One of these loyalists began Florida's first newspaper.

At the end of the American Revolution, the new United States returned the two Florida colonies to Spain, and most English settlers left. Saint Augustine became a Spanish city once again.

But Spain was losing its strength as a world power and wasn't able to protect and control its Florida colonies. Pirates continued to attack along the coast and American natives were involved in illegal trading with the new country to the north. United States citizens began drifting south into Florida as well. So many Americans moved to the east coast of Florida that by 1812 they tried to form their own Republic of East Florida. The War of 1812 had broken out between the United States and England, and in 1814 General Andrew Jackson captured Pensacola, using the excuse that Spain had permitted British ships to use the port. In 1819 Spain gave up what was left of its Florida colony. It became a U.S. territory in 1822 and finally a state in 1845.

Bibliography

Carpenter, Allan. *Florida*. Chicago: Children's Press, 1979.

History of St. Augustine, 1565–1702. St. Augustine, Fla.: Historic St. Augustine Preservation Board, 1987.

Jacobson, Daniel. *The Gatherers*. New York: Franklin Watts, 1974.

Judge, Joseph. "Exploring Our Forgotten Century." *National Geographic*, March 1988.

Lyon, Eugene. *The Enterprise of Florida*. Gainesville: University of Florida Press, 1976.

————. *St. Augustine, 1580: The Living Community*. St. Augustine, Fla.: El Escribano, 1977.

————. *Santa Elena: A Brief History of the Colony*. Research Manuscript Series, no. 193. Columbia, S.C.: Institute of Archaeology and Anthropology, 1984.

Manucy, Albert. *Houses of St. Augustine*. St. Augustine, Fla.: St. Augustine Historical Society, 1962.

May, Julian. *Before the Indians*. New York: Holiday House, 1969.

Milanich, Jerald T., and Susan Milbrath, eds. *First Encounters: Spanish Explorers in the Caribbean and the United States, 1492–1570*. Gainesville: University of Florida Press, 1989.

Quinn, David B. *North America from Earliest Discovery to First Settlement*. New York: Harper and Row, 1977.

Smith, James M. *Before the White Man: The Prehistory of St. Johns County, Florida*. St. Augustine, Fla.: Historic St. Augustine Preservation Board, 1985.